Whole 3

Whole 30 Diet Cookbook

Simple, Healthy & Delicious Weight Loss Recipes For Beginners

Table Of Contents

Introduction..5

Chapter 1: Understanding the Whole 30 Diet.............................6

Important Things to Consider...7

The Prohibited Food List..8

Chapter 2: The Whole 30 Diet Kitchen 10

The Essential Kitchen Tools..11

Convenient Kitchen Tools...12

Whole 30 Diet Meal Planning...13

Chapter 3: Beef and Pork..14

Simply Special Grilled Steak...14

Sausage Patties with Caramelized Onion and Mashed Sweet
     Potato..16

Beef Brisket...18

Pork Chops and Applesauce..20

Mama's Chili...22

Crunchy Pork Tenderloin...24

Chapter 4: Eggs and Poultry 26

The King's Favorite Scrambled Eggs..26

Tomato and Spinach Frittata 28

Salmon in Eggs Benedict...30

Chicken Meatballs 32

Chicken Primavera 34

Chicken Cacciatore 36

Chapter 5: Soups and Curries 38

Oriental Cold Cucumber Soup 40

Western-style Hot Cucumber Soup 42

Leek and Parsley Soup...43

Scallop and Tomato Curry...47

Chapter 6: Seafood 49

Roast Fish with Olives and Crisp Sweet Potatoes.........49

Simple Crab cakes 51

Roasted Herb Salmon..53

Spanish-style Shrimp 54

Grilled Tuna and Slow-cooked Onions 55

Citrus and Ginger Halibut 57

Chapter 7: Side Dishes..59

Roasted Brussels Sprouts and Sweet Potatoes with Balsamic
        Sauce..59

Stir-fried Shiitake Mushrooms 61

Simple Steamed Broccoli...62

Lemon and Garlic Cabbage Slaw...63

Creamy Cauliflower Mash 65

Easy Tomato and Basil Salad 67

Special Cauliflower Rice...68

Conclusion 70

Introduction

Discover amazing tips and recipes for the Whole 30 Diet.

The Whole 30 Diet is a diet program that will help you train your mind and body to choose healthy, simple whole foods. It eliminates the types of food from your diet that cause skin problems such as acne, digestive issues such as the leaky gut syndrome, chronic allergies, and hormonal imbalance. Think of this diet program as a way to help your body cleanse itself so that traces of these problem-causing foods will be flushed out of your system. As a result, you will be able to absorb nutrients from your meals better, thus your body becomes more nourished, fit, and healthy.

In this book you will find guidelines on how to do the Whole 30 Diet, including practical tips on how to set up your kitchen and buy your food supplies. More importantly, you will find a variety of recipes for delicious, inexpensive, and healthy meals that are easy to prepare at home. Choose from the different beef, pork, poultry, eggs, soups, curries, seafood, and side dishes to create your daily meal plans for the Whole 30 Diet.

You can start the Whole 30 diet any time. You can even begin right now!

Let's begin the journey.

Chapter 1: Understanding the Whole 30 Diet

There are so many diets out there, your head would just spin if you attempt to try them all. However, the bottom-line should always be to nourish your body and help it function properly. An ideal diet would be one that promotes eating healthy whole foods that are rich in vitamins, minerals, and unprocessed macro nutrients, namely carbohydrates, protein, and fat. One diet that will help you with that is the Whole 30 Diet.

The Whole 30 Diet is so named because it is a diet program that aims for you to eat only whole foods for 30 consecutive days. The purpose of the diet program is to eliminate traces of consumed compounds from the body that cause gut problems, hormonal imbalance, and inflammation. These compounds are found in sugar, grains, alcohol, legumes, and dairy products.

Those of you who are serious about completing the Whole 30 Diet would be happy to know that it stands by the principle of simple eating. In other words, your food preparation skills do not have to be likened to a five-star restaurant chef. You can prepare the meals easily at home in your own kitchen, with tools that you may already have. This is the perfect diet program for people who have a busy schedule and do not have a lot of time to prepare their food.

Important Things to Consider

The Whole 30 Diet will require you to eliminate a list of foods from your meals for an entire month, so you need to brace yourself. Anticipate and prepare ahead for food cravings, particularly for the ones that have been banned. Consider the fact that the benefits far outweigh the sacrifices that you have to make.

Before beginning any type of diet, make sure to consult a medical professional. Not everyone can adjust to a diet as restrictive as the Whole 30 Diet, and people with existing medical conditions such as diabetes and high blood pressure should always refer to their doctor's prescription.

In this diet program, you can eat all the fruits and vegetables that you like, as long as they do not fall under the *prohibited* category. You can also enjoy a variety of (preferably organic) meat, seafood, and eggs. Nuts, seeds, and healthy fats and oils are also encouraged in the diet because of all the healthy nutrients that only they can provide.

At the start of the Whole 30 diet, it is recommended that you weigh yourself and take note of your weight. After completing the program, weigh yourself once more. Do not ever weigh yourself during the program because your focus should be on eating clean and not on how much you weigh or even how you look. The purpose of weighing yourself before and after is to show you measurable results from the effort that you put into improving your lifestyle.

To add flavor to your meals, you can still use all forms of herbs and spices, most types of vinegar (such as balsamic, white, red wine, and apple cider), and of course, sea salt and freshly ground black pepper.

The Prohibited Food List

This list is a lot shorter compared to the list of foods that you can eat. Instead, it would be better for you to keep this list as you make your food selections. These foods are prohibited for a good reason: they are the culprits behind slow metabolism, fast weight gain, chronic inflammation (including skin and gut problems), and allergies. This is because these foods are not considered as natural by the body, that is why your system is reacting so negatively to them. Here is the list:

- All types of sugar. Not even the so-called natural ones maple syrup, honey, coconut sugar, and agave nectar. Instead, use juice freshly extracted from fruit as your sweetener.

- All forms of alcohol and tobacco products.

- Vinegar containing sugar and malt

- All grains. Some common grains are wheat, barley, rye, corn, oats, millet, rice, sorghum, buckwheat, bulgur, amaranth, and even quinoa.

- Most legumes, such as all sorts of beans (no black, white, red, kidney, pinto, and so on), chickpeas (sometimes called garbanzo beans), peas, peanuts, and lentils. This would naturally mean you should avoid all forms of peanut butter and soy products, such as miso, tempeh, tofu, soy sauce, and lecithin. The only legumes that you can still enjoy are snow peas, green beans, and sugar snap peas.

- All dairy products, such as cheese, yogurt, milk, sour cream, kefir. Only ghee and clarified butter are regarded as acceptable.

- All food products that contain sulfites, MSG, and carrageenan.

- All pseudo junk food and baked goods that are found in Paleo recipes. This means you should eliminate Paleo-style pancakes, bread, muffins, and so on.

As you can see, the Whole 30 Diet is not for the faint of heart; you still need to summon an impressive amount of willpower to be able to pull through it. At first, it might be a challenge. After all, old habits die hard. But the more dedicated you are to this 30 day diet, the easier it will be for you. Make your goal as clear as can be: you need to nourish your body with clean, healthy food so that you can perform optimally, look your best, live longer, and feel great.

Before you embark on your Whole 30 Diet journey, surround yourself with positive vibes and invoke a can-do attitude. Think of the next 30 days as a gift to your body and mind; you love yourself that is why you are willing to make sacrifices for the sake of your health. Always remind yourself that all the effort you will put into planning your grocery shopping, food preparation, and meal schedule will be worth it in the end.

Believe that you can and you will be able to go through the Whole 30 Diet program. You are doing this because you deserve to look and feel healthy and happy. And during the biggest of challenges, take comfort in the fact that by the end of this 30 day diet program, the best version of yourself will emerge.

Chapter 2: The Whole 30 Diet Kitchen

The right kitchen setup is essential to effectively follow any type of diet program. An ill-equipped kitchen will make it so much easier for one to give into temptation and start cheating. Spend a few hours to give your kitchen a face lift and prepare it for the Whole 30 Diet. After all, you will be doing this for 30 consecutive days, so the time spent on prepping your kitchen is worthy of the investment.

The first thing to do is to clear your kitchen and remove all foods that fall under the *Prohibited* category. Donate them to the nearest soup kitchen or pack them up in a box (just make sure that they will not spoil in there in the next 4 weeks). After that, clean up the kitchen until it is sparkly clean. Display *only* the items that are required by the Whole 30 Diet in food preparation; keep everything else hidden in a shelf or packed away in a box and stored in the attic. You will want to reduce as much clutter as possible so that preparing food becomes stress-free; it might even be enjoyable.

The Essential Kitchen Tools

You do not have to purchase new tools to do this diet program. If you do not have certain items that the recipes call for, then simply skip them and choose something else. The following is a checklist of items that you may want to keep within arm's reach in your kitchen:

✓ Cutting board(s); for safety reasons, you should have separate cutting boards for meat, vegetables, and bread

✓ High-quality knives, preferably 3 types: the chef's knife, the carving knife, and the paring knife; throw in a knife sharpener for good measure

✓ 3 or 4 pots, ranging from 1 quart to 4 quarts (depending on your needs); one with a steamer insert would be highly beneficial

✓ 2 skillets, preferably oven-safe or cast-iron; a non-stick skillet is also recommended

✓ 1 wok or saute pan with a cover

✓ A strainer, but if you can have 2, then pick one fine mesh strainer and one with big holes for steaming

✓ Measuring cups and spoons

✓ Baking sheets designed for roasting

✓ Baking paper

✓ A food processor and/or blender; if it is not possible for you to get any one of these, then prepare for a lot of chopping and dicing action in the kitchen

✓ A meat thermometer, for safety and flavor preservation reasons.

Convenient Kitchen Tools

This is a list of items that you may want to keep in the Whole 30 Diet kitchen, but they are not necessarily essential. Nevertheless, if you already have them then you should keep them around because they will make food preparation a breeze for you.

✓ Julienne peeler, for making vegetable noodles

✓ Garlic press, to make mincing garlic easy

✓ Meat tenderizer, for better quality meat dishes

✓ Zester and/or juicer, because plenty of recipes call for fresh lime, lemon, and orange juice and zest

✓ Grill basket, for easy vegetable and fruit grilling

Lastly, open up your kitchen and let natural light and air come in. If you cannot do that, then simply clear up the horizontal surfaces on your kitchen to make it appear more spacious and airy. If it is dim, light it up a bit more by installing a few more light fixtures. Small, inexpensive changes can make a big difference.

Once you have set up your kitchen, you are now ready to start planning your meals.

Whole 30 Diet Meal Planning

You alone can design the kind of meal plan that perfectly suits your lifestyle. You need to determine the days when you have absolutely no time to prepare food so that you can cook food in advance and store them in the refrigerator for quick and easy reheating. Plan your meals at least 3 days ahead of time, and this includes buying your needed ingredients at the grocery store.

To plan your meals, first decide how many meals you want to eat within each day. Let's say you want to have breakfast, lunch, dinner, and a light snack in between, so the next step would then be to choose the recipes for each type of meal. List down the ingredients that are being called for and adjust the amount per ingredient based on the number of servings that you want to prepare. Once you have your list of ingredients, add them to your grocery list and go buy them! If certain ingredients are not available or are not in season, simply ask the grocery staff for some recommended alternatives or use the internet.

At the grocery store, start with the eggs and meat section, then move on to the produce section to get your organic fruits, vegetables, and fresh herbs. If you are on a tight budget, you can opt for canned or frozen produce as long as they do not contain syrup.

Once you have bought all of the ingredients, pack them according to their recipes and store them properly. It would help if you bookmark a copy of the recipes for each meal in your mobile device or print out a hard copy and post it on the refrigerator or on your kitchen bulletin board.

In the succeeding chapters, you will find a variety of inexpensive and simple recipes that will fit wonderfully into your Whole 30 Diet Program.

Chapter 3: Beef and Pork

Simply Special Grilled Steak

Makes: 3 servings

Preparation Time: 30 to 40 minutes

Ingredients:

- 3 steaks, such as strip, tenderloin, rib eye, or sirloin, 5 oz each
- 2 shallots, peeled
- 3 garlic cloves, peeled
- 3 Tbsp extra virgin olive oil
- 1 1/2 tsp sea salt
- 1 1/2 tsp freshly ground black pepper
- 1 large avocado

Instructions:

1. Set the grill to 500 degrees F or the oven to 350 degrees F to preheat. Line a baking sheet with aluminum foil.

2. In a bowl, combine the salt and pepper, then use 2/3 of it to season both sides of the steaks.

3. On the prepared baking sheet, combine the garlic and shallots. Drizzle 1 1/2 tablespoons of olive oil and season with the remaining salt and pepper mixture.

4. Roast the garlic and shallots for 25 minutes, or until very tender. Transfer to a food processor with the remaining olive oil and puree. Transfer the mixture to a dish, cover, and set aside.

5. Place the steaks on the preheated grill and sear for 3 minutes, or until they can easily be removed from the grill. Flip over and sear for 1 to 2 minutes, depending on the preferred doneness. Set the steaks aside for 10 minutes.

6. Slice the avocado in half and remove the pit. Place the halves on the grill with the pitted side facing down. Grill for 3 minutes, or until golden. Scoop out of the skins..

7. Place the steaks on a platter and add the grilled avocado on top. Spoon the garlic and shallot mixture all over, then serve.

Sausage Patties with Caramelized Onion and Mashed Sweet Potato

Makes: 3 servings

Preparation Time: 50 minutes

Ingredients:

- 1 1/2 lb ground pork
- Grated zest of 1 1/2 lemons
- 1/3 tsp each of garlic powder, ground sage, onion powder, and dried thyme
- 1/6 tsp each of nutmeg and cayenne pepper
- 1 1/2 tsp sea salt
- 1/6 tsp freshly ground black pepper

For the Caramelized Onion and Mashed Sweet Potato

- 3 medium sweet potatoes, peeled and diced large
- 2/3 cup full fat coconut milk
- 6 Tbsp clarified butter or ghee
- 2 small onions, sliced thinly
- 1/3 tsp sea salt
- 1/3 tsp freshly ground black pepper

Instructions:

1. Set the oven to 350 degrees F to preheat. Line a baking sheet with baking paper and set aside.

2. Boil 6 cups of water in a pot over medium high flame.

3. In a bowl, combine the ground pork, lemon zest, spices, salt, and pepper. Mix thoroughly with your hands, then divide into 12 patties. Arrange on a tray and freeze for 15 minutes.

4. Place the sweet potatoes into the boiling water and cook for 15 minutes or until fork tender. Drain and place the sweet potatoes back into the pot.

5. Stir in 1 1/2 tablespoons of clarified butter or ghee in the sweet potatoes, then pour in the coconut milk. Mash well until thoroughly combined. Cover the pot with a lid and set aside.

6. Take the sausage patties out and arrange them on the prepared baking sheet. Bake for 15 minutes, or until the meat thermometer shows 145 degrees F and the patties are cooked through.

7. While the patties are baking, place a skillet over medium flame and melt the remaining clarified butter or ghee. Tilt the pan to coat evenly. Once hot, stir in the onion and cook for 15 minutes, or until caramelized and browned.

8. Spoon the sweet potato mixture into a bowl and scrape the caramelized onion on top. Season with the salt and pepper and mix well. Serve the baked sausages patties with it.

Beef Brisket

Makes: 3 servings

Preparation Time: 4 hours and 30 minutes

Ingredients:

- 4 1/2 Tbsp cooking oil
- 2 1/4 lb beef brisket, trimmed
- 1 1/2 Tbsp sea salt
- 1 1/2 tsp freshly ground black pepper
- 1 onion, peeled and quartered
- 2 sprigs fresh thyme
- 6 garlic cloves, peeled
- 7 1/2 cups beef bone broth or filtered water

Instructions:

1. Set the oven to 350 degrees F to preheat.

2. In a bowl,combine the salt and pepper, then use it to season the brisket all over.

3. Place a Dutch oven or an oven-proof roasting pan over medium high flame and heat the cooking oil. Once hot, place the brisket into the pan and sear for 2 minutes per side or until golden brown all over.

4. Take the brisket out of the pan, then set heat to medium. Stir in the onion and cook as you scrape the bottom of the pan to loosen up the browned bits. Cook the onion for 3 minutes.

5. Add the garlic and cook for 1 minute. Stir in the thyme and broth or water, then add the brisket. Set to medium high flame and cook until boiling.

6. Once boiling, place the lid on the pan and carefully transfer it into the oven.

7. Bake for 3 hours and 30 minutes to 4 hours, turning the brisket once every hour.

8. Take the brisket out of the pan and place in a bowl. Shred with two forks and remove excess fat. Remove the thyme sprigs.

9. Cool the liquid from the pan to room temperature, then skim off the fat from the surface. Pour the liquid into a food processor or blender. Blend well, then pour back into the pan.

10. Place the pan over medium high flame and bring to a simmer. Simmer to a desired thickness.

11. Pour the sauce on top of the shredded brisket and serve, preferably with roasted sweet potatoes or carrots or butternut squash.

Pork Chops and Applesauce

Makes: 3 servings

Preparation Time: 25 minutes

Ingredients:

- 3 bone-in pork chops, approximately 1 1/2 lb in all
- 1 1/2 tsp sea salt
- 1 1/2 tsp freshly ground black pepper
- 4 1/2 Tbsp cooking oil
- 3 apples, peeled, cored, and diced
- 2 small onions, sliced
- 3/4 cup apple cider
- 2/3 tsp each of allspice and ground ginger
- 1/4 tsp nutmeg
- 1 1/2 cups baby greens, such as endives, arugula, baby spinach, or baby kale

Instructions:

1. Set the oven to 350 degrees F to preheat.

2. Combine the salt and pepper in a bowl, then sprinkle all over the pork chops.

3. Place a skillet over medium high flame and heat 3 tablespoons of cooking oil. Sear the pork chops in the skillet for 3 minutes or until golden brown. Flip over and sear the other side for 2 minutes.

4. Place the pork chops on a baking dish and roast for 12 to 15 minutes, or until the meat thermometer reads 140 degrees F.

5. Meanwhile, mix together the remaining cooking oil with the onion in the skillet. Place over medium flame and saute until the onion is translucent.

6. Place the diced apples, ginger, apple cider, nutmeg, and allspice into the skillet and saute for 5 minutes until the apples are very tender.

7. Set aside to cool slightly, then transfer to a blender or food processor and process until smooth.

8. Divide the baby greens among three plates. Place a pork chop on each plate and spoon the applesauce on top. Serve at once.

Mama's Chili

Makes: 3 to 4 servings

Preparation Time: 1 hour and 40 minutes

Ingredients:

- 1 1/2 lb ground beef or bison or lamb
- 3 cups beef broth
- 2 small red bell peppers, seeded and minced
- 1 green bell pepper, seeded and minced
- 5 garlic cloves, minced
- 21 oz diced tomatoes
- 2 small onions, minced
- 1 1/2 tsp each of chili powder and cumin
- 3/4 tsp each of sea salt, mustard powder, and paprika

Instructions:

1. Place a heavy-bottomed pot over medium high flame and heat up; do not add cooking oil.

2. Stir in the ground meat and saute for 10 minutes, or until browned and crumbled. Transfer the meat to a platter with a slotted spoon and set aside.

3. Saute the onion, cumin, paprika, garlic, chili powder, salt, and mustard powder in the oils from the ground meat in the pot. Set to medium low flame and saute for 5 minutes, or until onion becomes translucent.

4. Stir in the tomatoes, bell pepper, and then the broth. Set flame to high and bring to a boil.

5. Once boiling, reduce heat to low and let simmer, uncovered, for 1 hour. Stir in the ground meat and cook until heated through. Serve piping hot.

6. Alternatively, cook all the ingredients after Step 2 in a slow cooker for 8 hours on low heat.

Crunchy Pork Tenderloin

Makes: 3 servings

Preparation Time: 50 minutes

Ingredients:

- 1 1/2 lb pork tenderloin, outer skin removed
- 1 1/2 Tbsp each of onion powder, paprika, and garlic powder
- 3 Tbsp mustard powder
- 2 1/4 tsp each of sea salt and freshly ground black pepper
- 3/4 cup chopped walnuts
- 4 1/2 cups salad greens

For the Vinaigrette:

- 1 Tbsp balsamic vinegar
- 1 garlic clove, minced
- 1/2 tsp mustard powder
- 1 1/2 Tbsp extra virgin olive oil
- 1/4 tsp mince fresh cilantro or 1/8 tsp dried cilantro
- Sea salt
- Freshly ground black pepper

Instructions:

1. Set the oven to 375 degrees F to preheat.

2. Blot the tenderloin dry using paper towels.

3. In a bowl, combine the onion powder, mustard powder, garlic powder, salt, pepper, and paprika. Massage the mixture all over the tenderloin and set aside.

4. Crush the walnuts until ground in a food processor or using a mortar and pestle. Spread the walnuts on a flat surface and roll the pork tenderloin on it to coat 3/4 of its surface.

5. Transfer the coated tenderloin on a baking pan and roast for 30 minutes or until the meat thermometer reads 145 degrees F. Remove from the oven and set aside for 10 minutes.

6. Divide the salad greens among three plates. Prepare the vinaigrette by combining all of the ingredients for it in a bowl. Season with salt and pepper to taste, then whisk well and set aside.

7. Slice the pork tenderloin with a carving knife into half inch thick rounds. Arrange the rounds on top of the salad greens, then drizzle the vinaigrette on top and serve.

Chapter 4: Eggs and Poultry

The King's Favorite Scrambled Eggs

Makes: 3 servings

Preparation Time: 20 minutes

Ingredients:

- 3 Tbsp cooking oil
- 9 large eggs
- 1 small bell pepper, seeded and sliced thinly
- 1 small onion, minced
- 1 1/2 cups chopped greens, such as spinach, kale, or chard
- 1 1/2 cups sliced mushrooms, such as button, portabello, or cremini
- 1 large avocado, pitted, peeled, and diced
- 1/3 tsp sea salt
- 1/3 tsp freshly ground black pepper

Instructions:

1. Heat the cooking oil in a skillet over medium low flame. Tilt the skillet to coat its entire bottom.

2. Saute the onion, mushrooms, and bell pepper until onion is translucent. Add the greens and saute until wilted.

3. Beat the eggs in a bowl and then pour into the skillet, stirring and scraping until fluffy. Cook from 5 to 7 minutes, depending on your desired consistency.

4. Turn off the heat, then add the diced avocado on top. Season with salt and pepper, then slice and serve.

Tomato and Spinach Frittata

Makes: 3 servings

Preparation Time: 25 minutes

Ingredients:

- 9 large eggs
- 3 Tbsp cooking oil
- 1/3 tsp sea salt
- 1/3 tsp freshly ground black pepper
- 1 small onion, diced
- 12 oz baby spinach, chopped
- 1 1/2 cups seeded and diced tomatoes
- Zest and juice of 1/2 lemon

Instructions:

1. Put the oven on broiler or set to 500 degrees F to preheat.

2. Beat the eggs in a bowl and season with salt and pepper.

3. Place an oven-proof skillet over medium flame and heat the cooking oil. Tilt the skillet to coat its bottom evenly with the oil.

4. Saute the onion and tomato together until the onion is translucent and the tomato is tender.

5. Stir in the spinach and cook until wilted. Pour in the beaten eggs and spread evenly over the vegetable mixture.

6. Cook the eggs for 4 minutes or until the bottom side is firm; do not stir. Flip over and cook to a desired consistency.

7. Sprinkle the lemon juice and zest evenly on top, then place the skillet with the egg mixture into the preheated oven.

8. Broil 5 inches from the heat source for 5 minutes, or until the frittata is golden brown.

9. Remove the skillet from the oven, slice, and serve.

Salmon in Eggs Benedict

Makes: 3 servings

Preparation Time: 25 minutes

Ingredients:

- 3 skinless salmon fillets, 5 oz each
- 3 large eggs, poached
- 4 1/2 Tbsp cooking oil
- 1 1/2 tsp sea salt
- 2/3 tsp freshly ground black pepper
- 1/8 tsp cayenne pepper

For the Hollandaise:

- 1/2 Tbsp freshly squeezed lemon juice
- 2 Tbsp ghee or clarified unsalted butter
- 1 large egg yolk
- Sea salt
- Optional: Cayenne pepper

Instructions:

1. Set the oven to 350 degrees F to preheat.

2. Season the salmon fillets with salt and pepper on both sides.

3. Place a large oven-proof skillet over medium high flame and coat the bottom with cooking oil. Once heated, place the salmon fillets in, skinned part facing down.

4. Sear the salmon for 4 minutes, or until edges begin to firm up. Once they can easily be dislodged with a spatula, flip over and cook for 1 minute.

5. Place the skillet with the salmon fillets into the preheated oven and bake for 6 minutes.

6. Remove the salmon from the oven and set on a plate.

7. To make the hollandaise, place the ghee or clarified butter into a small saucepan and heat until warmed through; do not bring to a simmer. Remove from heat and stir in the egg yolk, lemon juice, salt, and cayenne pepper. Set aside.

8. Top each salmon fillet with a poached egg, then drizzle the hollandaise on top. Sprinkle a bit of cayenne pepper over each, then serve.

Chicken Meatballs

Makes: 3 servings

Preparation Time: 35 minutes

Ingredients:

- 1 1/2 lb ground chicken thigh
- 3 garlic cloves, minced
- 1/2 onion, minced
- 2 small eggs, beaten
- 1 1/2 tsp sea salt
- 2/3 tsp freshly ground black pepper
- 3 tsp minced fresh oregano or 1 1/2 tsp dried oregano
- 3 Tbsp cooking oil

Instructions:

1. Set the oven to 350 degrees F. Prepare a baking sheet by lining it with baking paper.

2. In a bowl, combine the ground chicken with the egg, salt, pepper, oregano, and garlic. Mix very well with your hands, then divide into 30 meatballs.

3. Place a skillet over medium high flame and heat the cooking oil. Once hot, cook the meatballs for about half a minute for each side, flipping over occasionally, until all the meatballs are golden brown. Cook in batches depending on the size of the skillet.

4. Place the meatballs onto the prepared baking sheet, then bake for 10 minutes, or until the meat thermometer reads 160 degrees F.

5. Set the meatballs aside for 5 minutes before serving. Best served with roasted vegetables.

Chicken Primavera

Makes: 3 to 4 servings

Preparation Time: 45 minutes

Ingredients:

- 3 Tbsp cooking oil
- 3 garlic cloves, minced
- 1 1/2 tsp fresh thyme
- 1 1/2 tsp minced fresh oregano
- 3/4 cup diced onions
- 4 1/2 cups seeded and diced tomatoes
- 1 1/2 cups boneless, skinless chicken thighs, diced
- 2 1/4 cups each diced yellow squash and zucchini
- 3 cups green beans, sliced into bite-sized pieces
- 1/3 tsp red pepper flakes
- 1 1/2 tsp sea salt
- 3/4 tsp freshly ground black pepper
- 3 Tbsp minced fresh basil

Instructions:

1. Place a Dutch oven or large, heavy-bottomed pot over medium high flame and heat the cooking oil. Tilt the pot to coat the bottom evenly.

2. Stir in the onion, garlic, thyme, and oregano. Saute until the onion becomes translucent.

3. Stir in the diced chicken and tomatoes. Saute for 4 minutes, or until tender.

4. Stir in the zucchini, squash, and green beans. Saute until vegetables are fork-tender but crisp on the outside and chicken is completely done.

5. Sprinkle the salt, pepper, red pepper flakes, and basil. Saute for half a minute, then serve at once.

Chicken Cacciatore

Makes: 3 servings

Preparation Time: 55 minutes

Ingredients:

- 6 Tbsp cooking oil
- 3/4 lb boneless chicken thighs
- 1 1/2 lb bone-in and skin-on chicken legs
- 1 1/2 cups chicken broth or filtered water
- 1 small onion, minced
- 3 garlic cloves, minced
- 1 small red bell pepper, seeded and diced
- 1 1/2 Tbsp capers, drained
- 1 1/2 cups mushrooms, sliced
- 21 oz canned diced tomatoes
- 1 1/2 Tbsp chopped fresh basil leaves
- 2/3 tsp each of sea salt and freshly ground black pepper

Instructions:

1. Place a skillet over medium high flame and heat 3 tablespoons of cooking oil. Tilt the skillet to cover the bottom.

2. Sprinkle the salt and pepper all over the chicken, then sear the chicken in the hot skillet for 3 minutes per side, or until golden brown. Transfer the chicken to a platter and set aside.

3. Set the skillet on medium high flame and heat the remaining cooking oil. Saute the onion and bell pepper for 3 minutes, or until onion is translucent. Stir in the mushrooms and saute for 2 minutes.

4. Stir in the garlic and saute until fragrant. Stir in the diced tomatoes and capers, then place the chicken back into the skillet.

5. Add the chicken broth or filtered water, then set heat to medium. Bring to a simmer, then set heat to low. Let simmer for half an hour, or until the meat thermometer reads 160 degrees F.

6. Sprinkle the fresh basil on top, then serve.

Chapter 5: Soups and Curries

Butternut Squash Soup

Makes: 3 servings

Preparation Time: 45 minutes

Ingredients:

- 4 1/2 Tbsp ghee or coconut oil or clarified butter
- 4 1/2 cups peeled, seeded, and diced butternut squash
- 6 cups chicken broth
- 3 garlic cloves, minced
- 3/4 cup diced onion
- 1 1/2 tsp sea salt
- 3/4 tsp freshly ground black pepper

Instructions:

1. Place a soup pot over medium flame and melt the fat or oil. Tilt to coat the bottom evenly.

2. Stir in the onion and saute until translucent. Stir in the ginger, garlic, and butternut squash. Cook until garlic is fragrant.

3. Stir in the chicken broth and increase heat to high. Bring to a boil, then reduce to a low boil. Cook for 10 minutes, or until the butternut squash is very tender. Turn off the heat.

4. Cool the soup to room temperature, then process in a blender or food processor. Pour the soup back into the pot and reheat over medium high flame. Season to taste with salt and pepper.

5. Serve the soup warm, preferably with hard-boiled eggs, grilled chicken, or steamed greens.

Oriental Cold Cucumber Soup

Makes: 2 servings

Preparation Time: 30 minutes

Ingredients:

- 1 large cucumber
- 1 1/2 cups chicken broth, chilled
- 1/2 small chili, stemmed, seeded, and minced, or 1/8 tsp cayenne
- 1 1/2 Tbsp coconut aminos
- 1 1/2 Tbsp white wine vinegar
- 1/4 cup minced trimmed scallions, white and green parts
- 1/2 cup chopped fresh mint, cilantro and/or Thai basil
- 1/2 cup chopped arugula or watercress

Instructions:

1. Peel and slice the cucumbers in half, then remove the seeds with a spoon. Slice into extra thin pieces using a mandolin, if possible.

2. Place the cucumber slices in a bowl, then add the coconut aminos, white wine vinegar, and chili or cayenne. Mix well, then refrigerate for 20 minutes.

3. Take the bowl of cucumber out of the refrigerator and stir in the chilled chicken broth, scallions, and watercress or arugula.

4. Season to taste with salt, then place in the refrigerator and chill. Top with herbs before serving.

Western-style Hot Cucumber Soup

Makes: 2 servings

Preparation Time: 30 minutes

Ingredients:

- 1 large cucumber
- 3/4 cup chicken broth, chilled
- 1/2 cup chopped watercress
- 1/2 cup chopped fresh mint or dill
- 1 shallot or red onion, minced
- 3/4 cup coconut cream, chilled
- Sea salt
- Freshly ground black pepper

Instructions:

1. Peel and slice the cucumbers in half, then remove the seeds with a spoon. Slice into extra thin pieces using a mandolin, if possible.

2. Place the cucumber slices in a bowl and add a teaspoon of salt. Toss gently to coat, then refrigerate for 20 minutes.

3. In a bowl, combine the chilled chicken broth, coconut cream, shallot or onion, watercress, and a dash of black pepper. Toss in the cucumber slices and chill until ready to serve.

4. Before serving, top with fresh mint or dill.

Leek and Parsley Soup

Makes: 3 servings

Preparation Time: 50 minutes

Ingredients:

- 1 Tbsp extra virgin olive oil
- 4 cups chicken or vegetable broth
- 2 garlic cloves, minced
- 1/2 yellow onion, diced
- 1 leek, white and light green parts, halved and sliced thinly
- 2 parsnips, peeled and sliced into half inch thick diagonal pieces
- 1/2 tsp ground cumin
- 1/2 Tbsp grated fresh ginger
- 1/3 tsp sea salt
- 1 Tbsp apple cider vinegar
- 3/4 cup shredded kale leaves

Instructions:

1. Place a heavy bottomed pot over medium low flame and heat the olive oil. Stir in the leeks, garlic, and onion. Saute for 10 minutes, or until leeks are browned.

2. Stir in the parsnips and cook for 20 minutes, or until light golden brown.

3. Stir in the cumin and ginger and cook for half a minute. Add the chicken broth and increase heat to a boil.

4. Once boiling, reduce heat to medium low and simmer for 20 to 30 minutes.

5. Stir in the shredded kale and season to taste with salt. Cook until kale is partially wilted. Stir in the apple cider vinegar and remove from heat. Serve at once.

Cauliflower and Chicken Curry

Makes: 2 servings

Preparation Time: 40 minutes

Ingredients:

- 1 Tbsp cooking oil
- 1 lb cauliflower, chopped
- 1/4 cup minced onion
- 3 canned plum tomatoes with juices, sliced
- 1/2 lb boneless, skinless chicken, cubed
- Juice of 1/2 lemon
- 1 tsp curry powder
- Sea salt
- Freshly ground black pepper
- Optional: 1/2 Tbsp cumin seeds
- Optional: minced fresh parsley or cilantro

Instructions:

1. Place a skillet over medium high flame and heat the cooking oil. Cook the onion, sauteing occasionally, for 5 minutes, or until browned.

2. Stir in the curry and cumin seeds, then cook for half a minute. Set flame to high and add the cauliflower. Saute for 1 minute, then add the sliced tomatoes with the juices and 2 tablespoons of water. Mix well.

3. Season with salt and pepper, then place the lid on the skillet and reduce to medium low flame. Cook for 10 minutes, stirring occasionally.

4. Once the cauliflower is tender, stir in the chicken and cover. Cook for 6 minutes, or until the chicken is cooked through. Add more water, if needed.

5. Add the lemon juice and season again to taste. Remove from heat and add the fresh herbs. Serve at once.

Scallop and Tomato Curry

Makes: 2 servings

Preparation Time: 25 minutes

Ingredients:

- 1 lb large sea scallops
- 1/2 Tbsp cooking oil
- 2 medium ripe tomatoes, seeded and chopped
- 1 Tbsp curry powder
- 1/4 cup coconut cream
- 1/4 cup chopped fresh cilantro
- Juice of 1/2 lime
- Sea salt
- Freshly ground black pepper

Instructions:

1. Place a nonstick skillet over medium flame and heat for 3 minutes. Meanwhile, season the scallops with salt and pepper. Place the curry powder onto a plate.

2. Add the oil to the skillet and, as it heats up, coat the scallops in curry powder and then place on the pan. Cook the scallops for 2 minutes per side, or until browned all over.

3. Once all the scallops are browned. Stir in the coconut cream and tomatoes. Cook until heated through. Season to taste with salt and pepper.

4. Remove from heat and stir in the lime juice and cilantro. Serve at once.

Chapter 6: Seafood

Roast Fish with Olives and Crisp Sweet Potatoes
Makes: 2 servings

Preparation Time: 40 minutes

Ingredients:

- 1/2 lb sweet potatoes, peeled
- 1/2 cup black olives
- 1/4 cup extra virgin olive oil
- 7 bay leaves
- 1 lb monk-fish fillets or other similar fish fillet
- Sea salt
- Freshly ground black pepper

Instructions:

1. Set the oven to 400 degrees F to preheat. Slice the sweet potatoes thinly and set aside.

2. Coat a large baking pan with half of the olive oil, then arrange the sweet potato slices in it, overlapping slightly. Season with salt and pepper, then arrange the bay leaves on top.

3. Drizzle the remaining olive oil on top of the sweet potatoes, then roast for 8 minutes.

4. Gently shake the pan to stir up its contents, then roast for an additional 8 to 10 minutes, or until sweet potatoes are browned.

5. Arrange the olives and fish fillets on top of the sweet potatoes, then season with salt and pepper. Roast for 10 minutes, or until the fish is cooked through. Serve at once.

Simple Crab cakes

Makes: 6 servings

Preparation Time: 1 hour

Ingredients:

- 1 1/2 lb fresh lump crab meat

- 2 small eggs, beaten

- 2 Tbsp mustard powder

- 6 Tbsp extra virgin olive oils

- 1 lemon, sliced into wedges

- Sea salt

- Freshly ground black pepper

Instructions:

1. In a bowl, season the crab meat with salt and pepper, then add the egg and 1/2 tablespoon of mustard powder. Mix well, then cover with plastic wrap and place in the freezer for 5 minutes.

2. Shape the crab meat mixture into 6 even patties. Place a sheet or plastic wrap on a platter and arrange the Crab cakes on it. Cover with another layer of plastic wrap.

3. Refrigerate the patties for at least half an hour.

4. Spread the remaining mustard powder on a platter.

5. Heat the oil in a large skillet over medium flame.

6. Lightly dredge the crab patties in the mustard powder, then cook them in skillet for 6 minutes per side, or until browned and cooked through.

7. Serve the Crab cakes with the lemon wedges and your favorite side dish.

Roasted Herb Salmon

Makes: 2 servings

Preparation Time: 30 minutes

Ingredients:

- 2 Tbsp ghee or clarified butter
- 1 lb salmon fillet
- 2 Tbsp minced parsley or dill or chervil
- Sea salt
- Freshly ground black pepper
- 1 lemon, sliced into wedges

Instructions:

1. Set the oven to 475 degrees F to preheat. Put the butter and 1 tablespoon of herbs in a roasting pan and place the pan in the oven for 3 minutes.

2. Season the salmon with salt and pepper, then place it in the hot pan with the skin side facing upward. Roast for 4 minutes.

3. Take the pan out of the oven and peel off the salmon skin. Season with salt and pepper, then flip over.

4. Roast for 5 minutes, more or less depending on your preferred doneness.

5. Spoon the butter and herb mixture on top of the fillet, then top with the remaining herbs. Serve with the lemon wedges.

Spanish-style Shrimp

Makes: 2 servings

Preparation Time: 20 minutes

Ingredients:

- 1 lb shrimp, (optional: un-shelled for more flavor)
- 2 1/2 Tbsp extra virgin olive oil
- 1/2 tsp ground cumin
- 1/2 tsp paprika
- 2 large garlic cloves, sliced into slivers
- 2 Tbsp chopped fresh parsley leaves
- Sea salt
- Freshly ground black pepper

Instructions:

1. Pour the oil into a skillet and add the garlic. Place the skillet over medium flame and cook until the garlic starts to sizzle. Once sizzling, stir in the paprika and cumin.

2. Set heat to medium high, then stir in the shrimp and season with salt and pepper. Cook until shrimp is cooked through.

3. Turn off the heat, then stir in the parsley and serve.

Grilled Tuna and Slow-cooked Onions

Makes: 2 servings

Preparation Time: 45 minutes

Ingredients:

- 1 1/2 Tbsp extra virgin olive oil
- 1 lb tuna fillet
- 3 onions, sliced thinly
- 1 medium tomato
- 1/4 cup chopped black olives
- 1 fresh thyme sprig or dried thyme
- Sea salt
- Freshly ground black pepper

Instructions:

1. Heat the olive oil in a large skillet over medium flame. Saute the onion with the thyme and a dash of salt and pepper.

2. Saute onion until sizzling, then reduce heat to the lowest setting. Cook for 20 minutes, or until very tender; do not brown.

3. While the onion is cooking, chop the tomatoes and remove the seeds. Squeeze out excess liquid, then dice.

4. Prepare a grill to maximum heat and attach the rack 4 inches above the heat.

5. Season the tuna with salt and pepper on both sides, then grill for 3 minutes per side, turning only once.

6. While grilling the fish, add the olives and tomatoes into the skillet with the onions. Increase the heat and stir for 6 minutes, or until tomatoes are extra juicy and tender. Season to taste with salt and pepper.

7. Transfer the onion mixture onto a platter, spreading evenly. Place the grilled tuna on top, then serve.

Citrus and Ginger Halibut

Makes: 3 servings

Preparation Time: 35 minutes

Ingredients:

- 3/4 cup apple cider

- Juice of 1 large orange

- Juice and grated zest of 2 large lemons

- 3/4 tsp ground ginger or 3/4 Tbsp of grated fresh ginger

- 4 1/2 Tbsp cooking oil

- 3 halibut fillets, 5 oz each (or cod, haddock, striped bass)

- 1 1/2 tsp sea salt

- 3/4 tsp freshly ground black pepper

Instructions:

1. Set the oven to 400 degrees F to preheat.

2. Pour the apple cider into a saucepan and place over medium high flame. Simmer for 5 minutes or until it is reduced to approximately 1 1/2 tablespoons.

3. Stir in the lemon and orange juices and ginger. Simmer for 5 minutes or until it is reduced to half its original volume. Turn off the heat and stir in the lemon zest. Set aside.

4. Place a large skillet over high flame and heat 3 tablespoons of the cooking oil. Tilt the skillet to coat the bottom.

5. Season both sides of the halibut fillets with salt and pepper, then place the fish with the top side facing down into the hot skillet. Sear for 3 minutes.

6. Meanwhile, line a baking sheet with baking paper and grease the paper with half of the remaining cooking oil.

7. Take the halibut fillets out of the pan and arrange them in a single layer on the prepared baking sheet, seared side facing up. Coat the top of the halibut fillets with the remaining cooking oil.

8. Bake for 12 minutes, or until the fillets can easily be flaked using a fork. Place a on a platter and drizzle the citrus ginger glaze on top. Serve at once.

Chapter 7: Side Dishes

Roasted Brussels Sprouts and Sweet Potatoes with Balsamic Sauce

Makes: 3 servings

Preparation Time: 30 minutes

Ingredients:

- 1 1/2 cups balsamic vinegar

- 2 small sweet potatoes, peeled and cubed

- 4 1/2 Tbsp melted ghee or coconut oil or olive oil or clarified butter

- 5 garlic cloves

- 1 small red onion, sliced thinly

- 3/4 lb Brussels sprouts, trimmed and halved

- 2/3 tsp sea salt

- 1/3 tsp freshly ground black pepper

Instructions:

1. Set oven to 400 degrees F to preheat. Prepare a baking sheet by lining it with baking paper.

2. Pour the balsamic vinegar into a saucepan and place over medium high flame. Bring to a boil, then reduce to a simmer. Simmer for 20 minutes or until the balsamic vinegar is thickened and reduced to half its original volume.

3. Turn off the heat and set the saucepan aside to allow the balsamic sauce to cool to room temperature.

4. Place the sweet potato cubes inside a bowl and add the 1 1/2 Tbsp fat or oil. Toss to coat, then spread the mixture on the prepared baking sheet.

5. Melt the remaining fat or oil in a skillet over medium high flame. Tilt the skillet to coat the bottom of the skillet. Stir in the Brussels sprouts and cook for 4 minutes, or until browned.

6. Stir the onion and garlic into the skillet and cook for 1 minute. Season to taste with salt and pepper.

7. Transfer the Brussels sprout mixture to the baking sheet with the sweet potatoes. Spread everything evenly, then roast for 16 minutes, or until the sweet potatoes are golden brown and fork tender.

8. Transfer the mixture to a platter and spoon the balsamic sauce on top. Serve with your favorite main dish.

Stir-fried Shiitake Mushrooms

Makes: 2 servings

Preparation Time: 25 minutes

Ingredients:

- 2 Tbsp extra virgin olive oil
- 1/2 lb shiitake mushrooms, trimmed and sliced
- 1/2 tsp minced garlic
- Sea salt
- Freshly ground black pepper
- Optional: 1/2 Tbsp chopped fresh parsley

Instructions:

1. Heat the oil in a skillet over medium flame. Add the shiitake mushrooms and season with salt and pepper.

2. Saute the mushrooms for 12 minutes, or until tender.

3. Stir in the garlic and set flame to high. Cook for 10 minutes, stirring occasionally, until mushrooms are crisp and browned.

4. Adjust seasoning to taste, if needed, then top with parsley and serve at once with your favorite main dish.

Simple Steamed Broccoli

Makes: 2 servings

Preparation Time: 20 minutes

Ingredients:

- 1/2 lb broccoli, tough parts trimmed off
- Juice from 1 lemon
- Extra virgin olive oil
- Sea salt

Instructions:

1. Boil salted water in a steamer and add the broccoli. Steam for 8 minutes, or until tender and bright green.

2. Transfer the broccoli into a colander and rinse under cold running water.

3. Drain the steamed broccoli thoroughly, then place inside a bowl. Season with salt and add freshly squeezed lemon juice and a drizzle of extra virgin olive oil. Toss well to coat

4. If desired, reheat over medium flame before serving.

Lemon and Garlic Cabbage Slaw

Makes: 3 servings

Preparation Time: 20 minutes

Ingredients:

- Juice of 1 1/2 lemons
- 2 garlic cloves, minced
- 1 large head green cabbage, shredded thinly
- 1/3 cup extra virgin olive oil
- 3 Tbsp chopped cashews
- 1 1/2 Tbsp chopped fresh basil
- 1 1/2 cups shredded carrots
- 3/4 tsp sea salt
- 3/4 tsp freshly ground black pepper
- 1 1/2 tsp sesame seeds

Instructions:

1. In a bowl, combine the lemon juice and garlic. Gradually drizzle in the olive oil as you mix until everything is thoroughly combined.

2. In a big bowl, toss together the cabbage, sesame seeds, carrots, and cashews. Add the lemon and garlic oil and toss well to coat.

3. Season to taste with salt and pepper, then toss in the basil. Serve at once with your desired main dish.

Creamy Cauliflower Mash

Makes: 3 servings

Preparation Time: 25 minutes

Ingredients:

- 6 cups chopped cauliflower florets
- 3 Tbsp clarified butter or ghee
- 3 garlic cloves, minced
- 1 1/2 Tbsp minced fresh parsley
- 3/4 cup coconut cream
- 3/4 cup chicken broth
- 1 1/2 Tbsp minced fresh parsley
- 1 1/2 tsp sea salt
- 1/3 tsp freshly ground black pepper

Instructions:

1. Heat 3 cups of water in a pot over medium high flame. Once boiling, place the cauliflower florets and garlic in. Let simmer for 15 minutes, or until the florets are fork tender. Drain and set aside to cool slightly.

2. Place the cauliflower into a food processor together with the salt, pepper, coconut cream, and clarified butter or ghee. Process until smooth, adding the chicken broth gradually.

3. Place the parsley into the food processor and blend together with the mash. Serve at once or warm over medium flame before serving. Serve with any of your favorite main dishes.

Easy Tomato and Basil Salad

Makes: 2 servings

Preparation Time: 10 minutes

Ingredients:

- 2 ripe medium tomatoes, seeded and chopped
- 1 cup chopped fresh basil
- Extra virgin olive oil
- Sea salt
- Freshly ground black pepper

Instructions:

1. Arrange the chopped tomatoes on a platter. Add the basil on top.

2. Season to taste with salt and pepper. Drizzle the olive oil all over, then serve.

Special Cauliflower Rice

Makes: 3 servings

Preparation Time: 20 to 25 minutes

Ingredients:

- 6 cups chopped cauliflower florets
- 3 garlic cloves minced
- 1 small onion, minced
- 4 1/2 Tbsp clarified butter or ghee
- 2 small carrots, peeled and finely diced
- 1 1/2 Tbsp minced cilantro
- 3/4 cup chicken broth
- 3/4 tsp sea salt
- 3/4 tsp freshly ground black pepper

Instructions:

1. Put half of the cauliflower florets into a food processor and pulse until you get a grainy consistency similar to rice. Transfer to a bowl and repeat with the remaining cauliflower. Set aside.

2. Place a large skillet over medium flame and heat the ghee or clarified butter. Tilt the skillet to coat the bottom evenly.

3. Saute the carrot and onion for 3 minutes, then add the garlic and saute for 1 minute.

4. Stir in the cauliflower rice and saute until heated through and thoroughly combined. Pour in the chicken broth and cover the skillet.

5. Steam for 12 minutes, or until fluffy but not mushy.

6. Turn off the heat and stir in the chopped cilantro. Season to taste with salt and pepper. Serve with your favorite main dish.

Conclusion

I'd like to thank you and congratulate you for transiting my lines from start to finish.

I hope this book was able to help you to plan and prepare meals in the Whole 30 Diet. The next step is to stick to the program and enjoy the benefits of eating clean and healthy food.

I wish you the best of luck!

To your success,

John Web

Printed in Great Britain
by Amazon